HAND OVER HAND OVER
THE EDGE OF THE WORLD

HAND OVER HAND OVER T

PATRICK SWANEY

EDGE OF OF THE WORLD

YESYES BOOKS

HAND OVER HAND OVER THE EDGE OF THE WORLD
© 2025 BY PATRICK SWANEY

NO AI TRAINING: Without in any way limiting the author's exclusive rights under copyright, any use of this publication to "train" generative artificial intelligence (AI) technologies to generate text is expressly prohibited. The author reserves all rights to license uses of this work for generative AI training and development of machine learning language models.

COVER & INTERIOR DESIGN: ALBAN FISCHER
PROJECT LEAD: KMA SULLIVAN
AUTHOR PHOTO CREDIT: STACY PETERS

ISBN 978-1-946303-01-1
PRINTED IN THE UNITED STATES OF AMERICA

PUBLISHED BY YESYES BOOKS
1631 NE BROADWAY ST #121
PORTLAND, OR 97232
YESYESBOOKS.COM

KMA SULLIVAN, PUBLISHER
KARAH KEMMERLY, MANAGING EDITOR
GALE MARIE THOMPSON, SENIOR EDITOR, BOOK DEVELOPMENT
ALBAN FISCHER, GRAPHIC DESIGNER
JILL KOLONGOWSKI, MANUSCRIPT COPY EDITOR
JAMES SULLIVAN, ASSISTANT EDITOR

for my mom and dad

CONTENTS

1

Search Party · 3
Extraction · 4
Brand New · 5
My First Apartment on the Second Floor · · · · · · · · · · · · · · 6
Commute · 7
If You Were an Electrician · 8
Dress Rehearsal · 9
Testimony · 11
Frame · 12
What We Want · 13
The Performance · 14
Shadows · 15
Picture Window · 16
An Exchange · 17
Cannonball · 18
Uncovered · 19
Sleepless · 20
If It's All the Same · 21

2

Waiting for an Airplane, Costa Rica · · · · · · · · · · · · · · · · · 25
Late Summer · 26

Consignment 27
That Kind of Party 28
Chipped Teeth 29
Sunday Morning 30
Tiny Living 31
Photograph 32
Wealth 33
Thief 34
For Example 35
Fading Flags 36
The Story of Mr. Kitchen 37
Another Celebration 38
Forecast 39
Immovable 40
Hand Over Hand 41

3

Field Trip 45
Today Is a Perfect Day to Fly a Kite 46
Falling Down 47
Selective Service 48
How to Turn the Moon into a Flashlight 49
Thermometer 50
The Wishing Well 52
Territory 53
If I Am Older then We Must Be Aging 54
Erosion 55

The Truth about Holding Hands 56
The Dance Hall 57
Misunderstanding 58
Stick Figures 59
In Plain Sight 60
Haints 61
Rain Check 62

Acknowledgments 65

"I knew that nothing stranger
had ever happened, that nothing
stranger could ever happen."

—ELIZABETH BISHOP

"Sometimes what looks like teleportation is just someone
running really fast through a tunnel."

—*THE ATLANTIC*, November 2022

SEARCH PARTY

The search party found his disappearance disappointing. It was over within an hour when the boy was spotted in plain sight on a park bench, humming and happy, with a magnifying glass around his neck and a balloon in his hand. "This just won't do," the search party said. The boy looked up at the faces surrounding him then looked up at his balloon. "I'm not supposed to talk to people I don't know," he said, swinging his feet. "It's like you were barely missing at all," the search party said. "Perhaps you need more time, a head start. Are there any mineshafts near here? Uncovered wells? You could be swept downriver. Maybe hitchhiking? Do you know any strangers?" They were excited now with the possibility of salvaging the search. "But it's up to you. Make it a surprise. Make it dangerous. We'll close our eyes. We'll count to a hundred. We won't peek." "I probably should go home," the boy said, hopping down from the bench. "No, don't tell us," the search party shouted. "We'll find you." But the boy was already crossing the street, his balloon bobbing behind him. "We'll find you," they repeated and closed their eyes as they began to count.

EXTRACTION

Mr. and Mrs. Dentist are not dentists. Mr. and Mrs. Dentist dig holes in their back yard. They feel better when they are digging, so they dig. Mr. and Mrs. Dentist have problems. They also have perfect teeth and smiles like cupcakes, so the world doesn't take their problems seriously. The Dentists want to live serious, adult lives. They want to shed the feeling that they aren't meeting expectations. They want to be in on the joke, but the world just laughs and returns their smile in a polished reflection they can't quite place, an image amplified like a flash bouncing off a perfect tooth or moonlight echoing off the wall of a well-dug hole. And so they continue digging. Mr. and Mrs. Dentist dig because it is the opposite of being buried. They dig to find bottom. They dig because a hole has no bottom until the digging stops. They dig on winter nights after long days in the world. They pick and scrape and chip at the frozen ground, working carefully around rocks, shoveling out cold bricks of dirt. They peel off their clothes until pale steam rises from their skin. They dig deeper until their bodies sweat and breathe. Until they feel better. Until their holes are shoulder deep and only their naked heads are above ground. Two misshapen molars ready to be pulled from the world.

BRAND NEW

The man uncovers the warning in an empty lot between a tattoo parlor and a barbershop. It seems unclaimed. Things will be better now, the man thinks. He gathers the warning beneath his coat and brings it home to his wife. "What is it?" his wife asks. He passes the warning gently to her. "It's ours," he says and steps back to admire his new family. She cradles the warning. She brings it close and whispers softly, something the man can't hear. The warning is weak from years of neglect. It's fragile and in need of repair. Together, the new parents polish its floodlights and nurture its quiet cries. They move the warning into their bedroom and watch over it as it sleeps. They make it their own. One morning his wife wakes up fast. "Listen," she says, "I think something is wrong." "Yes, I think so too," the man says. "Isn't it wonderful."

MY FIRST APARTMENT ON THE SECOND FLOOR

The manatees in my bathtub show no signs of leaving. They roll around the tub in slow maneuvers and release blubbering cries that sound suspiciously like mating calls. In the sink, sea foam spits from the drain. Low tide pulls sand across the ceramic bowl. A tiny sailboat, with tinier sailors, negotiates the dicey waters looking for a place to trigger the anchor, and I'm pretty sure a large-scale fishing operation is underway. I can't leave the apartment; the manatees may be in danger. My landlord calls to tell me there have been complaints. When I tell him about the uninvited seascape in my bathroom, he says he should be able to fix it. I'm not so sure, but he comes by the next day anyway to have a look. "I can't fix it," he says. I shrug. He shrugs. "Don't worry," he says, "this sort of thing happens all the time." The manatees bellow from the bathroom. Water spills down the hall and over the carpet; it pools around our feet. "This sort of thing happens," he repeats, and, together, we watch my furniture begin to float, the way everything surfaces when a shipwreck settles.

COMMUTE

On Thursday nights, just off Highway 17, there's a little league game well protected from the dark. I stop because I want to be part of my own American dream. Inside the bubble of light, in the bleachers along the first base line, a woman opens a red cooler and offers me a beer. "Thanks," I say. We watch the boys shift in the field, the kind of constant motion that if I let my eyes go out of focus looks like standing still. The traffic doesn't reach us here, just the chatter of the game. "I was on my way home," I say. "That's my son," she says, and points to one of the small bodies illuminated in the outfield. We drink. "I was at work," I say, and then, again, "I was just on my way home." I try to make this sound precise, but out here, between stretches of nothing, where no one stays for long, it feels unnecessary. She turns and smiles at me. "I was looking for something," I say. There's a final out. The game is over. The teams line up to walk past one another and slap hands. The woman packs up her cooler and joins the other parents in herding children toward the parking lot. They drive away. I drive away. All of us flickering, the pine trees, the slatted light.

IF YOU WERE AN ELECTRICIAN

I didn't think people used hammers to fix things anymore. So when I'm walking home from work and see a man tied around the waist to the top of a streetlight swinging hard against the unpainted steel, I'm surprised. The noise of his repair work stutters into the summer twilight. I stop and join the crowd that has already gathered. I watch the snap of his arm and see the sound of his hammer slide out along the skyline, tinting the air green, dissolving as it meets its reflection. Or maybe it travels down the pole, through the cracked sidewalk to where I'm standing, and if I try hard enough I can capture that lonely sound in my knees. The streetlight starts to flicker as the man keeps up a regular rhythm. "How's it going tonight?" I shout. The crowd shifts, uneasy about my interruption. He pauses. "It's getting dark," he says, then resumes hammering. The crowd begins to thin. But I stay, hoping to see his silhouette puncture the night.

DRESS REHEARSAL

In the middle of downtown, in the middle of the lunch hour sidewalk I take my shirt off. Then my shoes. My pants. I look up past the tall buildings and close my eyes. I want to be weightless. I wait. People push past me. I pull one sock off and feel a buoyancy beneath my bare left foot. A bubble forming between me and the world. I tug at the other sock and in my mind I'm already floating. Rising like a fleshy balloon. "Wait," a woman says, grabbing my wrist. Her small basement apartment is nearly empty. We face each other. With her blue eyes, blue dress, and blue cowboy boots she looks a little like the sky. I'm in my underwear. "There's too much light," she says. And I see her apartment is cluttered with light. A single light bulb on the ceiling overwhelms the room. Piles of light. Stacks and stacks of random, unorganized light spilling from the corners. "I want to be weightless," I say. I look up at the low ceiling, the fiery bulb: both impossibly far away. She squints her blue eyes as if she might cry but starts talking instead. She tells me her story, tragedy by simple tragedy. As she speaks, she slowly undresses. The blue dress, strap by strap, zipper, a clasp, pulling it gently to the floor. Blue cowboy boot. Blue cowboy boot. Unhurried as her life unfolds. She stops and we're both in our underwear. "I don't feel any better," she says. "I know," I say. I take her by the wrist. We move her rocking chair to the middle of the cluttered room. "Keep me steady," I say. I climb carefully onto the chair and reach for the light bulb. With each turn my fingers glow red. "Better?" I ask. "A little," she says. And we stay there for a moment, in the semi-dark, clasped at the wrists, while I rock ever so slightly two feet above the ground.

TESTIMONY

I can tell you that the man had a beard and wore glasses, that he stood with his arms crossed over his belly near the middle of the slow street, barefoot, in shorts and a t-shirt, looking up through the morning with purpose. "Look at that," the man said to me. He kept his arms folded and his head back, so I tried to look as he looked until I settled on a bird in a nearby tree. Honestly, it didn't seem all that remarkable. "It's a woodpecker," the man said. "Really," I said, what kind?" "Oh, I don't know about that," the man said, "but it's got a name." We watched in silence; I can't tell you for how long. The woodpecker lifted from its branch and was gone. The man too turned to go. "Yeah, it's got a name," he assured me.

FRAME

Remember the morning I rose early from a dream and put my head through our bedroom window? Forehead first. The glass popped and shattered, somehow leaving only a head-sized hole. The morning air rushed in like an earache, but you didn't wake up. We were living in that one-bedroom basement apartment below the landlord. I remember looking at the hole, studying it. Sitting in the dark, looking out at the dark for a long time. I felt uneasy. I felt blood and pulled a few shards of glass from my scalp. I kissed your cheek and still you slept. When you finally woke up, I had to tell you what happened. I explained the hole, explained the glass, my forehead, my blood on your pillow. I couldn't tell what you were thinking. Together we covered the hole with black electrical tape because that's all we had. Remember? We sealed it tight, sticky layers inside and out, until it seemed strong. I guess we both knew it was only temporary.

WHAT WE WANT

The coat rack, skinny and handsome, called out from across the cluttered thrift store. I was there specifically to replace my toaster, it having come to a fiery end that morning, when the coat rack caught my eye. "Take me," it said, "I can see you're the type who keeps his corners clean. You have a spot for me. Buy me." I still longed for a working toaster but was pulled past the scattered appliance shelves until we were nearly touching, the coat rack and I. "I'll make you happy," it said. "But I only have one coat," I said, "and I keep that on a hanger in a closet. In fact, I have ample closet space. And what would you do in the summer?" "You can hang almost anything from my hooks. Please," the coat rack said, "I need you." "Can't you see how this will end?" I said. "Sure, we may make it work for a season or two, but then there will be feelings of neglect and remorse on my part, and feelings of neglect and inadequacy on yours; there will be cobwebs and jealousy, and we'll end up right back here. I just don't have room for all that. It's too much." I didn't know if the coat rack was shrinking or I was leaving. It got smaller and smaller until it was no larger than a chess piece. Still it called out; its voice thinned to a whisper. "Don't go," the coat rack said. I picked it up. It felt heavy, if not useful. At home I set the miniature coat rack in a clean corner of my front hall. I pulled my wool coat from a closet and, kneeling down, I delicately draped it from a single hook. "Oh, thank you," called the muffled coat rack. "I'm so happy."

THE PERFORMANCE

In a book of stories, I come across a character with my name. Same name, first and last. He wears a shirt with horizontal stripes and slipper-like shoes. He's a tightrope walker, a brilliant high-wire performer. His passion is to hover high above the ground, but not so high that he can't hear the crowd chanting his name, my name. His routine is practiced yet delicate. As he leaps and moves, both feet flutter over open space until the crowd believes he doesn't need the tightrope at all. But when he's not dancing on the high wire, this character with my name, he is horribly flawed. Strong from years of acrobatic training, he strangles people with lengths of cable cut from his act. Random people. With every murder the tightrope distance he loves so much is closing. The story might not be very good. Still, I'm strangely jealous. I envy his acrobat's good looks and the falling quality he has mastered. I see something in him that I don't see in myself, and for a moment my name is not me. I feel my feet on solid ground. I look down to see the lack of emptiness below.

SHADOWS

Because the instructions said a dark cool place with absolutely no sunlight and because the boy and girl were young enough to still believe in shadows, they buried the seeds in a shoebox and the shoebox beneath the basement stairs of her parents' house. Because the instructions said uninterrupted and six to eight weeks and because the boy and girl were young, they soon forgot about the shoebox and the two seeds planted inside and went about growing up. They grew up together at first and then grew restless and then grew apart. The girl moved away. The boy moved away. The girl's parents were already grown up, so they grew old and grew out of the girl's childhood home. When the girl returned to move her parents into a smaller home and found the buried box, she had forgotten the boy. Because she had forgotten when they buried the box together and were both young enough to believe in shadows, she opened it. It had been much too long. The two seeds had grown into two shadows and then become overgrown and then fused together in a lopsided pair. It was then the girl remembered the boy and felt the far-off weight of the boy's memory, a past inconsequential except that without it there would be no present. With no use for the shadows, the girl replaced the box where it had been buried. The house was sold, the girl went home again, the boy faded, and the shadows, because they were shadows, followed.

PICTURE WINDOW

Old men stop to press their faces to our window. They arrive as the sun sets. One by one an old man replaces another old man and night bends around them. Each owns a clumsy look, like a grandfather lost in his own driveway. Not helpless, not exactly harmless. We could turn away or close the curtains, but they'd be on the other side with their silence and open mouths and hands. So instead we watch. We stay up late. We keep quiet and the lights low. The old men shuffle toward their reflection with a disorganized curiosity. They pause and squint. We hold our breath, briefly, and there's a wrinkle where it's possible the old men have seen through the streaks and fingerprints, into our lives and found we have nothing they want. Eventually they wander off, puzzled, not remembering what it was they hoped for. And we remain unseen, behind our picture window, soothed by the open searching of each new face, waiting for morning when we can wipe the glass clean.

AN EXCHANGE

The man orders a coffee. The girl working the counter is pretty, the man thinks. Her hair is long, her arms are young, she smells like fruit and vanilla and cigarettes and mint. She smells like a memory, the man thinks. "You smell like a memory," the man says. Her mouth opens as if to respond. "It's a compliment," he says. The man tries to remember but can't. "All right," she says, but she's not looking at him. She looks toward the door, hoping for another customer. His coffee is ready. "I have a son about your age," the man says. He doesn't know why he says this; it's not true; he has no kids, isn't even married anymore, and the girl isn't listening. He puts a dollar in the tip jar. "Have a good one," she says mechanically. He fiddles over the cream and sugar wanting not to leave. He is sure about the memory if he could only remember.

CANNONBALL

Today we all have to pull our own cannon. We walk the bridge single file, a cannon tethered tight to every left ankle. Our line is daunting and slow, disappearing into the distance. Ahead of me is a father, behind me his daughter, such a large cannon for such a small girl, and I'm the stranger separating family. We all march together, methodical, lurching. The cannons are bright and freshly forged, but still the air smells of sulfur, an extinguished match. Nobody speaks. The cannons are quiet. The bridge is endless. When the rain comes, as it must, the bridge becomes slippery and the cannons begin to slip silently over the side. Our group is thinning. The cannon in front of me spills over the edge and the father, as he must, follows into nothing. Behind me his daughter is a witness; she tries to swallow, but sound escapes her chapped lips and rushes up the length of the bridge in a shiver of limbs, rain, and cannon. I pause in the gap where the father used to be, listening for an echo.

UNCOVERED

"Look how loose your skin is," the woman says, and grabs hold at his elbow. She pulls and the skin stretches, so that even though there is less of him there's more. "I don't see the problem," the man says. He thinks of his hunger like a bright spot on his tongue. A bright spot sliding down his throat. She collects his skin in folds. "Look at this," she says, with an armload of pasta-like elbow skin. A bright spot in his stomach. She is enveloped in elbow skin, but still she pulls. "How much more?" she asks. A bright spot expanding until there's nothing left. "Patience," the man says.

SLEEPLESS

The tumble of drinks and conversation is enough to wake me. The man and his pet possum are back on my porch. This is the third night in a row. I'm carrying my flashlight, but I flip the outside switch anyway, with what I hope is authority, and the porch goes quiet. Somehow, I feel like I'm interrupting. The possum is in my rocking chair his tail wrapped around a cigarette. He smokes casually. The man clutches to the railing, nearly upside down. I squint at the scene. The amount of bourbon left in the bottle tells me it's late. "It's late," I say. "I was sleeping." I ask the man and his possum to leave. The man tries to answer but his upside-down words come out garbled. The possum gives me a glowing look that tells me they will not. I point the flashlight at each of them, but the effect is lost in the illuminated porch. "Come on, this is unreasonable," I say. The possum is unflappable. He takes a drag off his cigarette and pours the last of the bourbon. A breeze comes up ticking the tall grass against the railing. The man sways a little. The possum offers me the drink. I decline. All I want is my bed. "This is the last time," I mutter, as I latch the screen door.

IF IT'S ALL THE SAME

At night the man is dreamless, and everyday he wakes up feeling the same. Each morning is an imitation of yesterday's morning and the morning before that, yesterday's yesterday and so on. His wife's a doctor, but he's not really looking for a cure. And it's usually the same with her as well: Did you feed the cat yet? Maybe it's time to start looking for another job. What are your plans for the day? He endures these questions silently and keeps his eyes on his soggy cereal, until eventually she asks, will you ever grow up? And he says, you're the one who married me. And she says, I thought you could change. And he shouts, how am I expected to change if I always feel the same? And that wraps it up; they go their separate ways. She takes the train to work and an elevator to her office where she makes decisions for other people. He stays in the house and watches the neighborhood unfold through the kitchen window, where he sees the same people do the same things in a performance just for him. An old man with a cane retrieves his newspaper. A ponytailed woman organizes the clutter in her garage for a yard sale she never has. A jogger waves to the ponytailed woman. The ponytailed woman waves to the old man with the cane. Watching this, the man sometimes wonders about his wife. He tries to imagine her going about her day inside her routine: ordered, measured. He sometimes tries to imagine himself from inside this routine, but his imagined self is shapeless, incomplete. The man won't be bothered by this because this morning is just like any other, and this morning the man feels fine.

2

WAITING FOR AN AIRPLANE, COSTA RICA

The tour group is mostly t-shirts and souvenirs. The man with a laugh like Wisconsin wears a suit and a nametag and takes pride in his waiting. There's lightning in the distance but not the worrying kind. The girl from Florence, South Carolina says I should visit Florence, South Carolina. I say, I think I'm going home. She gets it. We all get it. I want to carry a beer somewhere and drink it. There's a blurriness to the windows. What direction from here are you? At the gate there's more security, luggage and passports and shoes, again. In Costa Rica, among other things, there are hummingbirds. The trouble with hummingbirds is that you won't even see the one that darts the inside of your ear like a flower, ruining your balance permanently. Well-meaning strangers will rush to your side to say, are you all right? Did you see that hummingbird? And you in a twirling heap toward the ground ask, where? Where?

LATE SUMMER

Maybe I'm not feeling particularly brutal today. All the girls in town who just don't give a fuck are singing along in passenger seats with the window down and their heads back and eyes closed behind sunglasses. All the boys who aren't driving are lifting weights. A friend wants to tell me the Belgian Franc is on the rise. Do you expect something of me? I ask. There is sickness in the places I've lived. There might be people in my life I don't love. I don't want any more of this talk. Somewhere the birds are the same color as the water, so even as they dot the panoramic coast they're invisible. Somewhere a girl shows up on a boy's front porch and says I simply had to see you this morning. I think I'll scratch the to-do list from every refrigerator so we can cradle our accomplishments, or maybe I've got plans to pull the leaves from the trees today, one by one, just to hurry the winter.

CONSIGNMENT

When I tell you I sold your tricycle, you say, "It's like you sold my childhood." "Tricycle," I say. "It's like I sold your childhood tricycle." Because that's what I did, sold it to a man for a sleeping pill. I've been awake for a week. I've been worried. I've been cleaning, organizing, chipping away at our lives. "But the tricycle wasn't yours," you say. "You weren't using it," I say. "But I loved that tricycle," you say. "You haven't ridden it since you were a child. You're much too large for such a childish thing." "That's not the point," you say. You're upset and want your tricycle back, but the man who bought it said it was for his granddaughter or said he was a collector or that he had a sleeping pill and so a deal was made. "We need the space," I say. "What space?" you ask. "We're running out of room," I say. "What room?" The sleeping pill is poised and compact in my palm, but I'm having second thoughts. I'm worried. "We can't live like this." I've been awake for a week and still there's so much to be done. "I can't believe it," you say, "my childhood." "Tricycle," I say. "Childhood tricycle."

THAT KIND OF PARTY

I go to the party wearing a strand of lights around my neck like a scarf. It turns out I'm the only one there wearing lights as a scarf and even though people tell me I look fabulous I feel self-conscious and regret my wardrobe choice.

I get drunk because it is a party and tell everyone these aren't my lights; they're borrowed from a friend. Yes, but do they work? they ask. I'm led to a corner where I spend the rest of the night against the wall tethered to an outlet.

People love the lights even more now and the party expands around me. The lights paint my face a strange color and the few bulbs that touch skin are painful but people keep bringing me drinks, clapping me on the shoulder, and complimenting me on my lights.

And I have to remind them that they aren't my lights, I only borrowed them from a friend.

CHIPPED TEETH

We could be strangers with heart-shaped buttons pinned to our skin. "Dance with me," she says. "Yes," I say. It's not a whisper. She hums a little. There could be religion or music between us, and we try deeply not to feel embarrassed. "I feel badly for you," she says, "always." "This is not my fault," I say. It could be. We press our ugly muscled hearts together.

SUNDAY MORNING

Outside, yet another rowboat crawls across the intersection. Its oars scar the chalked asphalt leaving a wake of splinters. A terrible grind and shriek spreads through the neighborhood and your enthusiasm grows along with the clatter. "What a perfect morning for a rowboat ride," you say. It's true, the streets are calm, the sun and dry weather are holding. No one is drowning. It seems like a perfect morning to do almost anything, but your mind is made up. So we push our rowboat away from the porch, down the sloping lawn. It thumps over the curb and into the street. We sit on opposite benches facing one another. The street smells like an oil spill. "Where will we go?" I ask, but my words are swallowed by the scraping whine that washes over us. Other rowboats are filled with young families or new lovers and a disagreeable kind of happiness. They wave when they pass and pantomime greetings, content, despite their halting progress, to spend the day pulling across town. "Where will we go?" I repeat. You turn and gesture excitedly. The noise is unbearable. I don't want to ask again.

TINY LIVING

The waking day and its flesh too often feels familiar. The chair you like to sit in. The cup I like to drink from. The world flashes into a flattened piece of light, briefly, before it fattens again. "Like a reclamation under a moon-white tent," you say. "Like an invitation," I say. This may be panic thrashing in shallow water. This may be a corner of dry lung; brittle, doubtful. I may wish you would once wait for me. Or that once you wouldn't. You say, "If only we all weren't alive so differently." I say, "We can do better." We can build mannequins, trace cutouts, draft proxies that will be backlit until the resemblance obscures our selves. Until the outline proves its point and the music is turned over in the margin and we will be far away and swimming before anyone can say losing streak or anything at all.

PHOTOGRAPH

The photograph of us, taken at arm's length, has hung framed near your bed long enough to become unremarkable. A memory that's been memorized and goes unnoticed. But tonight I can't sleep, so I nudge you awake. "You can't see your face anymore," I say, pointing at the picture. "What do you mean?" you say, tiredly. "It's like you weren't even looking at the camera," I say. "So?" "So it's different." "It's a photograph," you say, "photographs don't change." But I can see how you lean away from me, distracted. The November trees are ragged, and the water is flat and cold in the background, but now your head is turned almost completely and only a hint of your profile is visible. "It wasn't like this before," I say. "It's always been like this," you say, rolling over.

WEALTH

Even while sleeping the man worries that bricks are being stolen from his house and then sold for a profit. Sold to the kind of people who buy stolen bricks, in rooms of hats and cigarettes and bartering. He flails at the bedside lamp, certain that with the lights on he'll be able to see a fresh hole in his wall and a gang of handsome men loading bricks into the night, creating a new currency and going home to feed their brick-children with brick-bought food. Is this what keeps us apart? The man wants answers. His pockmarked walls grow weaker each morning. Eventually, the man decides to hide bricks beneath his mattress to protect what's left of his home, but the situation only worsens.

THIEF

The thief is on my roof again, taking measurements. At first, I was flattered by his attention to detail, the planning. He wanted what I had. It felt like a compliment. But recently his work has been flimsy and ill-disguised, more of a distraction than anything else. The weight of his irregular pacing and the rattling zip of his tape measure fill the house. It's too early for this. I climb his ladder to my roof, and find him sitting near the peak, hunched over a small notebook. We haven't officially met. I clear my throat. "Can I help you?" I say. "You're not supposed to be here," he says. "Where would I be?" I ask. He shrugs. "It's my house," I say. "We'll see," the thief says, and turns back to his notebook. I look out over the neighborhood. The morning is warm. The sky is brightening with an edge of sun. "You know, I wasn't always a thief," the thief says. "I used to be a salesman, door-to-door. I sold things people needed, and things they didn't know they needed." I consider this. "You're still a thief," I say. "Well," he says, "who we are now doesn't change who we used to be." "Maybe," I say. He shrugs again. "I've got work to do," he says. He shuffles to his feet. Standing up he looks smaller than I expected. He moves in pauses. I watch him fumble with his notebook and tape measure. "Can I help?" I say. "It's your house," he says, and kicks at a loose shingle. "Here," I say, and hold the end of the tape measure against the peak as he walks unevenly toward the edge.

FOR EXAMPLE

If you pointed your finger at me like it was a gun I would give up without a fight but you don't want to play along and insist on words instead of guns and these words slip from us like handcuffs from a magician's tiny wrists beneath a cape and bottomless hat and our magic has a stage and the stage has shadows and a false floor and a curtain that covers the audience who is restless and shifting and shuffling but refuses to applaud and their combined silence has speed and is heading for the exit pushing toward the county line following train tracks hoping to hitch a ride but the train's delayed or missing or both and the passengers are on foot some running some walking all wishing for a place to sleep instead they find silence like a collision in each small town they pass because we have all their words but lack imagination so your finger is not a gun it's just a finger and you keep talking and I keep my hands where you can see them.

FADING FLAGS

When he returned, I asked my spaceman what he had missed most. "Running downhill," he said. His voice rattled around his space helmet, and he sounded far away and sad. "Would you like to now?" I asked. "Yes," he said. I took him to the top of my best hill. "It's pretty high," he said. I laughed. The day fluttered in his shadow. "And steep," he said. He looked heroic and unsteady, propped up by the wind. "You could take off your spacesuit," I said. "You'd go faster." "What would people think?" he said. I considered the town below. "Nothing," I said. "Nothing at all," he sighed. He shifted inside his suit and took a tentative step then another. He pumped his arms and began to rumble down the hill. I watched as he gathered speed, the static of his suit echoing behind him metallic and green. He sliced into the dip near the bottom before it flattened out and eased to a stop. He turned and looked up at me. He looked small. He waved. I waved back.

THE STORY OF MR. KITCHEN

Mr. Kitchen was renting property to Mr. Curtis and his wife, a small house with some land next to his own. This was out in Limestone County. This was years ago. Mr. Curtis kept chickens, but he didn't keep his chickens out of Mr. Kitchen's corn. Mr. Kitchen stopped to see Mr. Curtis about this, again. He was driving home from town and had his grandchildren in the car. It was a Saturday. "Can I help you, Mr. Kitchen?" Mr. Curtis asked. "Well, Mr. Curtis," Mr. Kitchen said, "I have to ask you to pen your chickens; otherwise, I have to ask you and your wife to move on." It was summer, but the summer heat wasn't full yet. Mr. Curtis came down from the porch. Mr. Kitchen took a step or two away from his black car and his grandchildren. "I don't plan on penning my chickens," Mr. Curtis said. "You're going to have to leave if you don't," Mr. Kitchen said. The house and the car and the grandchildren and the men were near the top of the short driveway, not too far from the road. The road was empty. "You try and make me and I'll kill you," Mr. Curtis said. "Mr. Curtis," Mr. Kitchen said, "I don't believe you'd kill me over something like that." But Mr. Curtis pulled a pistol from behind his back and, just like that, shot Mr. Kitchen dead.

ANOTHER CELEBRATION

My love wears a red apron. I know this because today, when I see her on the street, downtown, she's wearing a red apron and carrying boxes that are surely gifts she's bringing home to me. Not wanting to ruin the surprise, I duck behind a sidewalk sandwich board. She turns a corner and disappears. The board advertises dollar beers. It is almost lunchtime, and my love doesn't expect me home until dinner. I sit at the empty bar blinking as my eyes adjust. "I'll have the special," I say, when the bartender comes over. She sets my beer in front of me on a small white napkin. "One dollar," she says. "That's great," I say. "Is this place new?" "We've been here." "In this same spot?" "Since before the war." "No kidding." The exposed brick walls do look old and dust on the top shelf bottles seems to confirm a steady existence. "In fact," she says, "we're celebrating an anniversary just next week." "Well, congratulations," I say. "I can't believe I've never been here before." "You'd be surprised," she says. "An anniversary," I say, "so business must be good?" "We do all right. We usually get busy around lunch. And, here you are." I sip my beer. "That's true," I say. It feels good to be part of so much history in the middle of the day. The bartender smiles at me, "Want another?" she asks, meaning another beer. "Ok, but I can't stay forever, my love is waiting for me."

FORECAST

Your birthday was overturned inside a snow globe. Clowns clung to the ceiling, balloons floated to the floor, streamers lay flat against the edges of the room. Visibility was low. An ice-cream cake lit up your face, so we shouted, Blow out the candles! You paused. There was a flash, a camera probably, and one by one you put your tongue against the flames, until only charred wicks remained. Guests made excuses and reclaimed gifts and tried to find the exits. When you told me you had wished for someone to tell you a secret, ashes spilled from your mouth. I don't know any secrets, I said. You said you could wait.

IMMOVABLE

You say cars are designed to drift to the right, slightly, to avoid head-on collisions. I'm not sure this is true; I wonder if something is misaligned, but we're not moving anyway. Traffic has stopped on the highway. It's OK, you say. We join the makeshift community that stretches and smokes and speculates in the July heat. Here we are. Up and back, two lanes of cars pointed in the same direction on the side of a mountain. I toe the rumble strips on the shoulder and knock some gravel into our lane. I feel fragile standing in a place not meant for standing still. I once spent a summer walking the highway as part of a survey crew, measuring the Michigan topography from Bridgman to Watervliet. We carried ten-foot levels and wore reflective vests; we counted our steps and grew accustomed to the traffic that didn't bother about our breakability, and so we didn't worry either. This is not the same. We are moving again, together, and we see the delay was a camper blown apart, cracked in half, scattering the contents of the traveling home. Oh, you say. A dress has caught on a mile marker. Pinned against the summer. It lifts with a small shadow, as if on a rocking chair, as we pass.

HAND OVER HAND

At the college they're reenacting famous plane crashes. It's a fundraiser. We all go. In the auditorium we're waiting for the first plane. The woman sitting next to me tells me a story I don't ask to hear. She tells me about a girl who lived in a town on a plateau and a man who came across the plains, all squint and callus, pulling a rope that stretched behind him to the horizon. At the center of town, the man placed the end of the rope at the waiting girl's feet and clapped the dust off his hands beneath a sun that could have been any sun, high and flat. The girl didn't know what to do with the rope. She asked the man, but the man didn't answer. He just retraced his steps and disappeared in the distance as if he was climbing over the edge of the world. The woman stops talking like it's the end of the story. What did the girl do? I ask. What? the woman says. The girl, I say, with the rope? Oh, I don't know, the woman says, she could have done anything. What does this story have to do with me? I say. I think they're starting, the woman says, and resituates herself in her seat. The auditorium darkens and a spotlight follows paper streamers of flame and smoke from a failed engine across the stage.

3

FIELD TRIP

The school children tumble past the church toward the museum, a long line of tiny people making their way in the morning. A woman on a bicycle, with what looks like a violin in the basket, steadies herself on the sidewalk. A hearse, dark and short, takes up two parking spaces along the curb. The children pass the church, and the woman passes the children, and the hearse stays comically still in a brief single-file parade beneath the late-summer trees. I'm on my way to work and can't stop to see what happens next, which is probably nothing. It probably means nothing at all. And the morning is good with children and the possibility of music.

TODAY IS A PERFECT DAY TO FLY A KITE

But I don't have a kite. I have an egg. The day is perfect nonetheless; clear skies, warm, just the right amount of wind, today anything might fly. I gather all my string, tie one end to my egg and toss it into the perfect day. Over my shoulder, it floats for a moment. I run. The string unravels in ribbons. My feet slap the asphalt. I run faster, furiously, knees high, one arm pumping, the other stretched above my head giving my egg the best possible chance. I can barely breathe. I've never run this fast in my life. I peek back over my shoulder. It's working. My egg is rising, definitely rising. I don't dare stop. The string is taut. The string has weight. My egg is flying. It must be flying. Everything is a kite. The day is perfect, but I slow down. I have to. My legs are cramping, and the road limps flatly in front of me. I'm coughing and sweating. How far have I run? Holding tight to the very end of the string, I turn to look. I shade my eyes from the perfect day and follow the string, so much string. I search the sky.

FALLING DOWN

"I'm going to let you in on a secret," the very, very old man said as he sat down across from me on the midday bus. "I remain balanced," he said, "by wearing an equal number of rings on each hand." He paused to let this information sink in. He didn't break eye contact. Then unsheathed his hands from his jacket pockets and, leaning across the aisle, rested them on my knees. I could only assume there were fingers underneath the mass of jewelry. "Go ahead and count them," he said, "exactly the same number on each hand." He was uncomfortably close to me, but his breath smelled like cough drops, which was somehow reassuring. "Go ahead." He nodded at his hands that stayed heavy on my knees. The bus rattled on, over potholes around fast corners, and the very, very old man sat perfectly still. "I haven't fallen down in nearly fifty years," he boasted. "I used to be, let's just say, inelegant, but now fifty years without a single stumble, not one misstep. Imagine that." I tried to visualize fifty years. I tried to see the very, very old man as an old man. I imagined him tumbling down marriages, rolling out of jobs, bruised and shaky. "Whenever I feel even a little unsteady," he continued, "I just add more rings." He patted my knees and his hands felt like sacks of pennies. He stood up as the bus jerked to a stop. "What do you think of that?" he said. He eased his armored fingers into his pockets. The doors opened and he danced lightly down the steps into the afternoon.

SELECTIVE SERVICE

Reports of threats prompted the town to call for its army. "Not now," the men said, "we have conversations to finish." "But there are threats," the town said, "they could be serious. There may be fighting." "This is no time for fighting," the men said. The paved streets carried people on foot and in cars and on bicycles away from the town and away from the men. In the distance, there was smoke or dust or some trick of sunlight and atmosphere. Perhaps there was no distance at all. "Please," the town said. "Please," the men said, "you can have the army but we're talking." The town seemed satisfied. It was, after all, the army they wanted. The army marched. The men talked. The town waited, expecting accounts of bravery and heroism. When no word came, they wanted to know what it meant. "Are we winning?" the town whispered. "We are," the men assured them.

HOW TO TURN THE MOON INTO A FLASHLIGHT

She wants me clumsy. I want her more clumsily. So we pull at each other from opposite directions thinking maybe we can make the other one bigger without anyone breaking. The moon has covered our bed and drawn lines on her face. She says, "I'll get sad if you ask me to, but I have to be up really early tomorrow." I say nothing. She falls asleep. I wait for the moon to set, hoping to see fewer shadows, but our bed is downwind from the city, downwind from the river and its bridges, downwind from headlights, all of it flashing at the edges until the night is featureless and smooth, until, even with the moon on her face, there is no night at all.

THERMOMETER

The wives fill thermoses with warm soup and line them up by the door for the husbands. The husbands work the night shift at the blanket factory. They collect their thermoses and carpool. One drives while the others try to guess the night's soup. It's always the same—homemade creamy cauliflower—but they guess anyway, and it's always a pleasant surprise. A cold winter means good business, and the blanket factory hums with the smell of freshly pressed blankets. The husbands trade their thermoses for hardhats and safety goggles and punch timecards. They work in the finishing section of the baby blanket production line. Baby blankets are plucked from the slow-moving conveyor belt and inspected for flaws: edges, seams, loose threads, stitching, embroidery. Then hand-folded and individually wrapped. The husbands have no babies of their own; they are not fathers. The wives are not yet mothers. The husbands do careful, tender work; each wrinkle smoothed twice, each fold delicate and crisp. They wait for the whistle and the surprise of warm homemade creamy cauliflower soup. But the whistle doesn't blow. Instead it is the fire alarm. The blanket factory is on fire. The blanket factory will burn down. The husbands are reluctant to leave their station before their break, but they do. They are reluctant to leave without the soup, but the factory fills with smoke. The wives are awake and waiting. The fire will spread. They know this, but it is still a surprise to watch the flames reach their homes. In the cold night, the blaze becomes a comfort, not exactly like a blanket or even soup, but certainly warm enough.

THE WISHING WELL

The way my grandfather told it the old chapel caught fire and the flaming steeple, when it fell, toppled directly into the well. The water evaporated sending a chimney of soot and steam back into the air, which in turn put the fire out. He told it so often that it became true. Imagine that, he would say laughing, came right up out of the ground. Now that's holy water. Then he would press a penny into my hand. Every time. When he died, we buried him in the cemetery behind the rebuilt chapel, not far from the old well. Imagine that. As far as I know he hasn't come up.

TERRITORY

He sent her framed flowers from the border, pressed Alaskan cotton and forget-me-nots on a velvet background. "Because they reminded me of the way you play piano," he wrote. He went to work photographing the topography from the tops of bright mountains and stayed safe. "Marry me," he wrote. She was a beautiful piano player. "Everyday we collide with other lives and think almost nothing of it," she wrote. She liked to go out to the Chicago train yard where she would imagine a silent movie playing inside of each car that could be carried away from the cluster of tracks through open country and clear skies. "Yes," she wrote, and waited. He returned without any of the war, they had a child and hung the framed flowers in the nursery and let their lives spill together. When they were not nearly old, she stopped playing piano, and a papery quiet settled on their home. He wanted to know why. "Why?" he asked. She thought about the piano: its wires that were not a cage, its keys with nothing to unlock. "The possible futures were too many to imagine," she said. He had the piano packed away and pulled the framed flowers from the wall because they reminded him of the way she used to play. They were old enough to know the music wouldn't return. He pressed her hands between his. "Is this better" he asked. She looked out the window at the surrounding absence like a train held in the middle of the country and imagined their lives.

IF I AM OLDER THEN WE MUST BE AGING

Today is my birthday and because it has been too long since I have bought anything I need to grow into, I go shopping. I dig through long racks of jumbled sale items for khakis that have to be rolled twice at the cuff and cinched at the waist; a braided belt pulled tight with plenty of belt leftover; a turtleneck that fits baggily with sleeves I push up past my elbows; just the right pair of sneakers, something sturdy with an extra inch or so in the toe, and laces that can be double-knotted. I make my purchase exchanging only a smile with the nice-looking young woman working the register. At home I put on my oversized outfit. I move around trying to break everything in. I stare at my full-length reflection. I feel small and mismatched. My sister calls. I ask her if she remembers how it felt when we were younger, the way we rode Big Wheels, endlessly racing in opposite directions, howling as we passed. Remember how fast we were? How if we timed it just right as the sun fell behind the trees we could circle the block one more time before we were called in. Remember? Of course, she says. My god, we must have been impatient, I say. She laughs and wishes me a happy birthday. I decide not to wear the new outfit to my birthday dinner. I undress, fold the clothes carefully, and wrap them back inside the plastic shopping bag. Standing on my tiptoes, I push it to the very back of the top shelf of my closet.

EROSION

The waitresses are driving downtown and putting quarters in the meters and walking into work. It seems like an afternoon for washing windows or, better yet, nothing at all, and you and I have plans for the evening. After the storm, islands up the coast are being tied together with new bridges where the old bridges used to travel, an experiment testing inevitability. How long must the shore sustain the ocean? Experts suggest ferries instead of roads, but this concession seems to admit impermanence and is unacceptable. I say the ocean is not a flood it's just the ocean. You say we are all experts trying to save the shore of our own little island. The truth is we don't know our future selves, and we're not good at making decisions for strangers. It's all just guessing. I guess we'll keep walking into the ocean amazed at our ability to not be crushed by so much water, and we'll keep building bridges and coming to work and putting money in the meter and saying I'll see you later.

THE TRUTH ABOUT HOLDING HANDS

We were at the raffle again, winning pretty much everything. Wasn't that nice? It was the fall festival, held on the playground near the swing set and plastic slide. Fifth grade pageant girls played four-square during intermission. Anyone could see how everyone there wanted a child. We won two. I hoped for a third. You leaned into my shoulder. I imagined we would live in the middle of the country where the landscape unfolds like newsprint in the winter. Live inside a tornado and watch rivers swallow street signs in the summer. Live pressed together between so much space. But the crowd had become sticky and more familiar. Bottle rockets went off behind our heads, a yellow whistle waving goodbye. The festival was nearly over. You pulled away. "Look," you said and pointed toward the gymnasium, "someone's on the roof." I followed this invisible line, but it was too dark for me to see much beyond your finger. "A child?" I asked. A groan went up from the crowd. They had drawn our number again.

THE DANCE HALL

The tuba band plays slow and loud and the women dance. The tuba band plays the one song they know. They play it again and again until the room smells like a spit valve or a hand job. The women are dressed in dance. They wear their movements like the tuba band wears their one song. The dance floor is dark with bodies. The air is filled with tuba. The band puffs and vibrates and presses valves with fat fingers. The walls shiver and chandeliers send baritone back to the band in perfect pitch. The women feel tuba rub up their arms and legs. The women close their eyes. The tuba band plays faster. The women begin to fall behind. The women want to not feel the slippery tuba on the back of their neck, to not feel the tuba in their chest when they breathe. They want to flee the dance floor for a soundless night, but the tuba band plays on.

MISUNDERSTANDING

Tonight the city must look like a furnace from above. The street is crowded with so many people that they slow into a single crawling mass. We sit at a table just off the sidewalk talking in pauses. My head feels like it's filled with speckled light, and you look pretty. "Tell me a story," you say. "Last night," I say, "I dreamed I was playing guitar on an empty stage and singing. The guitar had a crack in it where the music leaked out, but people came from everywhere just to hear my voice." "You don't play guitar," you say. And you're right. "It was just sleep," I say. The night is unsteady, and I can tell you want to leave. I put my head on the table and listen for a pulse. From this angle the crowd turns back into people, all of us separate.

STICK FIGURES

You were backlit by the morning sun by the time I got there. Your face looked singed and healthy. "It's over," you said. "All of it?" I asked. You held a grey-black piece of fire like a charm or a souvenir. You turned it over, passed it from hand to hand. You took the dull end and etched a single line on your forearm. "Close your eyes," you said. I hesitated. "Please," you said. I shut my eyes and watched the smudge of your silhouette fade against my eyelids. You rubbed soot over my face in circles, the leftover fire carving my skin. "You can open them now." The ash felt heavy on my eyelids. "What do you see?" "I don't see anything," I said. I coughed. "I can't see anything." Your hand became slippery on my cheek. "Not anymore," you said.

IN PLAIN SIGHT

"May I touch your foot?" I asked the man. I had taken a seat next to him on a bench near a small lake. The man sat cross-legged and barefoot. "May I?" I repeated. The man had perfect soles—unblemished, the skin taut and stainless. He must receive this request fairly often, I thought. "All right," the man said. I touched the bottom of his right foot. It felt cool and smooth. Like polished glass, flawless, and almost slippery. "It's beautiful," I said. "Thank you," the man said. A couple paddled a canoe. Ducks drifted near the muddy shore. It was a pleasant day. My fingers tingled from touching the man's sole. With soles like those, I thought, this man could walk on water. I imagined him with a running start from our bench to the lake; he would land on the water with a delicate splash and just keep going, skimming the surface, his feet like flat stones rippling past the ducks and canoe to the far shore where he would disappear into the trees. "Impossible," I said. "Crawling," the man said. "What?" I said. "I crawl everywhere. I haven't walked since I was a little boy." "Crawling?" I said. "Crawling. Look at my hands, my knees," he said. "And see, the tops of the toes drag some." His hands and knees were pocked and calloused, scarred, nubbed and raw in places. Had I not noticed before? The man himself looked weathered and stooped, perhaps from so many years spent so close to the ground. "But your soles," I said. "I know," he said. "Like you could walk on water," I said. "Yes," the man said.

HAINTS

We're on the last horse out of July trying to hold on. We've got time and hot weather and outside government buildings on the saddest block on the saddest street people line up to share cigarettes and injustice. They lean against the low wall as if they might want to stay. You lick your upper lip. The courthouse has been repainted. All that's left is In God We Trust. This could have been our frontier town. This must have been our fortune. Every coin painted with our faces. We push back against the small of the afternoon. We want to unclench our fists to find the tremor all along was just the teeth of summer letting go or digging in or maybe we've been swallowed. The streetlights hesitate. We don't bother. We're pulling apart at the centerline. We want the patter of the auctioneer to soothe us to sleep. We've got one take to get it right. The night is a wisp, a trail of sky carved right across your ear. We're chopping down and away. We want the tree rings of another morning and another. We want to see the light trapped on the surface of the river. Don't desert me. Don't desert me. Don't desert me.

RAIN CHECK

The steady drizzle failed to slacken. No one bothers to bring in the flag. We'll wait, cigarettes tucked back into pockets. The day hangs like a jaw broken on both sides, chin against its chest. It's simple, force equals mass times acceleration; power equals work done over time taken. Take your time. Someone in the crowd says, everything will be fine. A man does push-ups on the curb. We push past him. Coins scatter on the street and we all pause. Someone holds a sign: "700-800 criminals, 120 loose women, 14 gambling houses and 14 dance halls." Silver madness, the man with the sign says. Silver madness, the man with a chicken under his arm says. The day is the color of salt inside a coal sack. A secretary waves with her right hand, but it's not an actual wave; she just opens and closes her fingers as if she's trying to grab hold of an invisible electric fence that separates the crowd from more crowd, edges from more edges, cautionary. The day wearies. Oh well, someone says. Oh well.

ACKNOWLEDGMENTS

Thank you to the editors of the journals in which the following poems first appeared, sometimes in earlier versions.

Anomalous, "Sleepless"
The Bookends Review, "Shadows" and "Falling Down"
Bryant Literary Review "Waiting on an Airplane, Costa Rica," "Field Trip," and "Selective Service"
Conduit, "That Kind of Party"
Flash, The International Short-Short Story Magazine, "If You Were an Electrician" and "The Wishing Well"
Inch, "Consignment"
Indiana Review, "Search Party"
Map Literary, "Haints" and "Today Is a Perfect Day to Fly a Kite"
Matchbook, "Thief"
NANO Fiction, "Hand over Hand"
Painted Bride Quarterly, "Extraction"
Redivider, "For Example"
Six Little Things, "Wealth"
Southeast Review, "My First Apartment on the Second Floor" and "Late Summer"
Sundog Lit, "Territory" and "Thermometer"

This book traveled a long way before finding a home, and I was lucky enough at each stop to be surrounded by an incredible group of writers, teachers, and friends. Thank you to the communities at the University of Colorado, the University of North Carolina Wilmington, and the University of Ohio that left their mark on the poems in this collection.

Thank you to KMA Sullivan and YesYes Books. Many thanks.

Thank you to my sisters for being family even when we live far apart.

An extraordinary thank you to my mom and dad. This book would not exist without your love and support.

Thank you, finally and of course, to Hank, Sehr, and Stacy. You make all the days better.

PATRICK SWANEY is the author of *Hand Over Hand Over the Edge of the World* (YesYes Books, 2025). His poems have appeared in *Boulevard*, *Conduit*, the *Indiana Review* and elsewhere. He is an associate professor of English and writer-in-residence at Catawba College and lives in Winston Salem, North Carolina.

ALSO FROM YESYES BOOKS

FICTION

The Nothing by Lauren Davis
Girls Like Me by Nina Packebush
Three Queerdos and a Baby by Nina Packebush
Book of Exemplary Women by Diana Xin

WRITING RESOURCES

Gathering Voices: Creating a Community-Based Poetry Workshop
    by Marty McConnell

FULL-LENGTH COLLECTIONS

Ugly Music by Diannely Antigua
Bone Language by Jamaica Baldwin
Cataloguing Pain by Allison Blevins
Strange Flowers by Bryan Byrdlong
What Runs Over by Kayleb Rae Candrilli
This, Sisyphus by Brandon Courtney
40 WEEKS by Julia Kolchinsky Dasbach
Salt Body Shimmer by Aricka Foreman
Gutter by Lauren Brazeal Garza
Forever War by Kate Gaskin
Inconsolable Objects by Nancy Miller Gomez
Ceremony of Sand by Rodney Gomez

Undoll by Tanya Grae
Dead Boys in Space by Sara Youngblood Gregory
Loudest When Startled by luna rey hall
Everything Breaking / For Good by Matt Hart
Brine Orchid by Arah Ko
murmurations by Anthony Thomas Lombardi
Sons of Achilles by Nabila Lovelace
Otherlight by Jill Mceldowney
Refusenik by Lynn Melnick
GOOD MORNING AMERICA I AM HUNGRY AND ON FIRE
    by jamie mortara
Born Backwards by Tanya Olson
a falling knife has no handle by Emily O'Neill
To Love An Island by Ana Portnoy Brimmer
Another Way to Split Water by Alycia Pirmohamed
Tell This to the Universe by Katie Prince
One God at a Time by Meghan Privitello
I'm So Fine: A List of Famous Men & What I Had On
    by Khadijah Queen
If the Future Is a Fetish by Sarah Sgro
Gilt by Raena Shirali
Say It Hurts by Lisa Summe
Boat Burned by Kelly Grace Thomas
Helen Or My Hunger by Gale Marie Thompson
As She Appears by Shelley Wong

RECENT CHAPBOOK COLLECTIONS

Vinyl 45s

    carried / in our language by Tatiana Dolgushina
    Exit Pastoral by Aidan Forster
    Crown for the Girl Inside by Lisa Low
    Of Darkness and Tumbling by Mónica Gomery
    Phantasmagossip by Sara Mae
    Juned by Jenn Marie Nunes
    Year of the Sheep by Stacey Park
    Scavenger by Jessica Lynn Suchon
    Unmonstrous by John Allen Taylor
    Giantess by Emily Vizzo

Blue Note Editions

    Kissing Caskets by Mahogany L. Browne
    One Above One Below: Positions & Lamentations
        by Gala Mukomolova
    The Porch (As Sanctuary) by Jae Nichelle

www.ingramcontent.com/pod-product-compliance
Lightning Source LLC
Chambersburg PA
CBHW050015090426
42734CB00020B/3272